D1503324

Symphony No. 1
in C Minor, Op. 68

Johannes Brahms

DOVER PUBLICATIONS, INC.
Mineola, New York

Bibliographical Note

This Dover edition, first published in 1997, is a republication of music from Volume 1 of "Symphonien für Orchester," edited by Hans Gál, from *Johannes Brahms, Sämtliche Werke / Ausgabe der Gesellschaft der Musikfreunde in Wien*, originally published by Breitkopf & Härtel, Leipzig, n.d.

International Standard Book Number: 0-486-29797-7

Manufactured in the United States of America
Dover Publications, Inc., 31 East 2nd Street, Mineola, N.Y. 11501

CONTENTS

Symphony No. 1
in C Minor, Op. 68

(1855–76)

INSTRUMENTATION

2 Flutes [Flöten, Fl.]

2 Oboes [Oboen, Ob.]

2 Clarinets in A, B♭ ("B") [Klarinetten, Klar.]

2 Bassoons [Fagotte, Fag.]

Contrabassoon [Kontrafagott, K.-Fag.]

4 Horns in C, E♭ ("Es"), E, B ("H")–basso
  [Hörner, Hr.]

2 Trumpets in C, E, B ("H") [Trompeten, Trpt.]

3 Trombones [Posaunen, Pos.]

Timpani [Pauken, Pk.]

Violins 1, 2 [Violine, Viol.]

Violas [Bratsche, Br.]

Cellos [Violoncell, Vcl.]

Basses [Kontrabaß, K.-B.]

Symphony No. 1
in C Minor, Op. 68

Symphony No. 1

in C Minor, Op. 68

4

8

12

END OF EDITION